CLASHES IN THE WILDERNESS

THE COLONIAL WARS

English settlers unload supplies at Jamestown, Virginia, in 1607. In the next century, thriving colonies grew up along the Atlantic coast from Georgia to Maine.

CLASHES IN THE WILDERNESS

THE
COLONIAL
WARS

ALDEN R. CARTER

FRANKLIN WATTS
A Division of Grolier Publishing
New York London Hong Kong Sydney
Danbury, Connecticut

Cover: General Edward Braddock's doomed British army marches into the Pennsylvania wilderness in the summer of 1755.

Maps by William J. Clipson

Cover photograph copyright ©: North Wind Pictures, Alfred, ME

Photographs copyright ©: North Wind Picture Archives, Alfred, ME: pp. 2, 10, 12, 13, 18, 20, 24, 34, 39, 46, 54; Historical Pictures Service, Chicago, IL: pp. 14, 40, 44, 53; Schenectady County Historical Society: p. 17 ("The Schenectady Massacre," by Sexton); Essex Institute, Salem, MA: p. 27; Anne S. K. Brown Military Collection, Brown University Library: pp. 29, 38; The Olde Print Shop: p. 37; The New Brunswick Museum, Canada: p. 43; Fort Ticonderoga Museum: p. 48; The Bettmann Archive: p. 52; National Archives of Canada, Ottawa: p. 55 (C-361, by R. Short).

Library of Congress Cataloging-in-Publication Data

Carter, Alden R.
The colonial wars : clashes in the wilderness / Alden R. Carter.
p.   cm.—(A First book)
Includes bibliographical references and index.
Summary: Chronicles the history of the Colonial Wars, also called the French and Indian Wars, which gave the British control of North America.
ISBN 0-531-20079-5 (lib. bdg.) / ISBN 0-531-15654-0 (pbk.)
1. United States—History—King William's War, 1689–1697—Juvenile literature.   2. United States—History—Queen Anne's War, 1702–1713—Juvenile literature.   3. United States—History—King George's War, 1744–1748—Juvenile literature.   4. United States—History—French and Indian War, 1755–1763—Juvenile literature.   [1. United States—History—King William's War, 1689–1697.   2. United States—History—Queen Anne's War, 1702–1713.   3. United States—History—King George's War, 1744–1748.   4. United States—History—French and Indian War, 1755–1763.]   I. Clipson, William J.   II. Title.   III. Series.
E195.C37   1992
973.2—dc20   92-9906   CIP   AC

FRANKLIN WATTS
A Division of Grolier Publishing
**Sherman Turnpike
Danbury, CT 06813**

CONTENTS

FOR
TOM KINNEY

ACKNOWLEDGMENTS

Many thanks to all who helped with *The Colonial Wars*, particularly my editors, Reni Roxas and Lorna Greenberg; my mother, Hilda Carter Fletcher; and my friends Barbara Feinberg and Dean Markwardt. As always, my wife, Carol, deserves much of the credit.

ON THE RIM
OF EMPIRE

★

O N A drizzly morning in September 1759, two small armies—one in British red, the other in French white—met in a cow pasture before the high walls of Quebec, Canada. This battle on the edge of the North American wilderness lasted only fifteen minutes, but it signaled the end of nearly three-quarters of a century of war and changed forever the future of our continent.

No one can say for sure when the struggle for North America began. Great Britain built its first lasting settlement in North America at Jamestown, Virginia, in 1607. A year later, the French founded the capital of New France at Quebec. Separated by the wilderness, the French and British colonies lived in peace for many years. France and Britain had very different ideas about the future of North America. The French were mainly interested in trading with the Native Americans for furs. French explorers and traders pushed into the vast interior of the continent, claiming for their king the Great Lakes and all the lands drained by the huge St. Lawrence and Mississippi river systems. On paper, New France stretched from Hudson Bay to the Gulf of Mexico and from the Appalachian to the Rocky mountains. However, the French government allowed settlement in little of this vast area. Under the watchful eye of the royal governor, most of the colonists settled along the St. Lawrence from Quebec to Montreal. A few more lived in Acadia (today's Nova Scotia) and at small

French colonists and Indian guests celebrate at Port Royal, Acadia (Nova Scotia). While British colonists cleared farms and built towns along the Atlantic seaboard, French "inhabitants" founded a wilderness empire in Canada.

outposts scattered across the wilderness. When the wars in North America began late in the 1600s, the French in North America numbered fewer than 15,000.

By then the British colonies along the Atlantic seaboard from Maine (then part of Massachusetts) to the Carolinas had a population of nearly 250,000. Britain viewed America as a place where its poor and dissatisfied subjects could produce agricultural and forest products for the parent country. The British government promoted settlement and allowed the colonies considerable self-government under governors appointed or approved by the king. Although most of the colonists lived within a few dozen miles of the coast, Britain claimed all the land westward to the Mississippi River.

The overlapping land claims of France and Britain made little difference to the Native Americans in the great wilderness beyond the French and British settlements. The Native American population is hard to guess, but perhaps 300,000 Indians lived in eastern North America in the late 1600s. Scattered in small tribes, they lived by hunting, fishing, gathering wild plants, and, in some places, farming small plots of land. Because the French did not crowd the Native Americans and usually traded fairly, most tribes were friendly to New France. Many French fur traders married Indian women and adopted Indian dress. French missionaries settled among the tribes, teaching them the Roman Catholic religion and learning Indian ways. The

Unlike their wandering kin on the plains,
the Iroquois lived in permanent villages
with cultivated orchards and fields.

British colonists had less sympathy for Native American customs and more hunger for Indian lands. They rarely married Indians and made little effort to convert the tribes to Protestant Christianity. Except for the mighty Iroquois Nation, most of the tribes were hostile to the British.

The five (later six) Iroquois tribes lived in northern New York. Masters of wilderness fighting, they dominated other Indian tribes from western Massachusetts to Indiana and from southern Canada to Virginia. The Iroquois had a long-standing grudge against the French dating from a brush with the founder of New France, Samuel de Champlain (c. 1567–1635), who had defeated them with a few shots from the first firearm they had ever seen. The Iroquois traded to acquire muskets of their own and became a constant threat to New France.

Trouble smoldered in North America long before events in Europe set off the first of the Colonial Wars (often called the French and Indian wars). Geography and furs lay at the center of the conflict between New France and the British colonies. Rivers were the natural highways for settlement

The French explorer Samuel de Champlain
fires on a war party of Iroquois in 1609.

Indians bring furs to trade at a European
outpost. New France dominated the fur trade
through its control of the waterways reaching
into North America's vast interior.

and trade in the wilderness. Control of the St. Lawrence
gave the French an easy route to the Great Lakes and the
Mississippi, but the British colonists had no such conve-
nient waterway to the rich interior with its wealth of furs.
Instead, the steep, heavily wooded Appalachian Mountains crowded the colonies against the ocean.

The British began challenging the French along the only two water routes through the Appalachians. One route led west from the Hudson River above Albany, New York, up the Mohawk River, by portage and stream to Lake Oneida, and down the Oswego River to Lake Ontario—a distance from Albany of about 170 miles (275 km). The second led north across a portage from the Hudson to Lake George, along slender Lake Champlain, and down the Richelieu River to the St. Lawrence below Montreal—a distance from Albany of some 200 miles (325 km). For nearly a century, the British struggled to open these waterways while the French fought to keep them closed.

The wars began in the heart of Iroquois country near what is today Rochester, New York. The Iroquois competed with the French as agents in the fur trade, often attacking Indian tribes trading with New France. In the summer of 1687, the governor of New France, the Marquis de Denonville, led an army of Indians and French Canadians south to punish the Iroquois. The Iroquois scattered into the woods, leaving Denonville to burn some empty villages. French trespassing on lands claimed by Britain enraged the governor of New York, who encouraged the Iroquois to strike back. On an August night in 1689, 1,500 Iroquois warriors swooped down on the village of Lachine, a few miles west of Montreal. They massacred 200 French men, women, and children and set the frontier aflame.

WAR
IN THE
WILDERNESS

★

NOT LONG after the La-
chine massacre, a fierce old man arrived in Canada to bring
fire and death to France's enemies. The Count de Frontenac
(1622–1698) brought news of a great war in Europe. The
War of the League of Augsburg (in America, called King
William's War) opened a long struggle between France and
Britain for dominance in Europe and for colonies in America and Asia. In the early years, neither nation sent armies
to North America, depending instead on the settlers and
their Native American allies to fight the battles in the
wilderness.

To rally the Indians and the Canadians, King Louis XIV
appointed Frontenac governor of New France for the second time in the old soldier's long life. Frontenac was brilliant, proud, and brutal. He ordered New France's Indian
friends to ravage the New England colonies. In the winter
of 1690, a large war party of Indians and French woods-

men trudged south over the Lake Champlain ice. In the middle of a February night, they charged through the unguarded gates of the small settlement of Schenectady, New York. They killed sixty settlers—including a dozen children—burned the town, and carried twenty-seven prisoners away. It was the first of a long series of bloody raids. Salmon Falls and Durham, New Hampshire; Falmouth, Maine; Groton, Connecticut; and many smaller settlements soon lay in ashes.

Indians and French woodsmen attack the village of Schenectady, New York, in the winter of 1690 at the beginning of the Colonial Wars.

A French priest baptizes Native American
converts. The hatred between French Catholics
and British Protestants contributed to the
brutality of the early Colonial Wars.

There was great cruelty in the Colonial Wars. Whites
and Indians on both sides tortured, scalped, and killed
without mercy. French priests led Indian raids to destroy
the Protestant settlements of the British colonies, while
Protestant ministers preached terror against the Roman
Catholics of Canada. The bloodshed would last for de-
cades, the fear and hatred for generations.

King William's War became a long series of raids and

massacres along the frontier. Both sides tried to organize large expeditions but failed to accomplish much. In 1697, news arrived of peace in Europe, and fighting sputtered out in North America. Frontenac died the following year, leaving the fate of Canada to lesser people.

The peace was short-lived. In the summer of 1701, Britain and France went to war again. The War of the Spanish Succession, or Queen Anne's War (1701–1713), was a very large war in Europe but a small affair in North America. The French made a deal with the Iroquois that kept the New York frontier quiet, then sent their Indian allies to raid settlements in Maine, New Hampshire, and Massachusetts. The most infamous raid took place at Deerfield, Massachusetts, on a snowy night in February 1704. The town's guards were asleep, convinced that no one would attack in such poor weather, when about 200 Indians and 50 French Canadians slipped over the log walls of the stockade. With bloodcurdling screams and waving tomahawks, they stormed the houses. A few settlers managed to hold out until daylight behind bolted doors and shutters, but the attackers cut down 50 townspeople, took 100 prisoners, and burned half the village before disappearing into the woods.

In 1711, Britain finally sent a major expedition to conquer Canada and to put an end to the long years of terror in America. Many of the 6,000 soldiers in the fleet bound for Quebec expected to settle in Canada and had brought their

VANINGEN, SNYDER.

families along. Just inside the mouth of the St. Lawrence, the fleet lost its way in a fog and anchored dangerously close to the north shore. In the night, a strong east wind blew ten ships onto the rocks. A thousand men, women, and children drowned. Disheartened, the admiral ordered the fleet back to England.

The war in Europe ended in 1713, with Britain the clear winner. In the peace treaty, France gave up any claim to the rich fur-bearing region bordering Hudson Bay. Equally important, Britain took control of the island of Newfoundland and the peninsula of Nova Scotia, which together formed the jaws of a trap ready to snap shut on the vital St. Lawrence passage into the heart of New France.

Deerfield, Massachusetts,
is set aflame in 1704. No
village—English, Indian, or
French—could sleep peacefully
in the long years
of the Colonial Wars.

THE GREAT FORTRESS

T H E F R E N C H needed a stick to jam in the jaws of the trap. They had it in Cape Breton Island just north of Nova Scotia. In 1720 they began building the mightiest fortress in North America on the east coast of the island. Named for the French king, Louis XV, Louisbourg took more than twenty years to construct and drained much of the gold from the French treasury. Yet by 1740, the French were well satisfied with the cost. The walled city carried on a brisk, although illegal, trade with New England. Ships passed in and out of the harbor by the hundreds in the shadow of high stone walls bristling with cannons. Two smaller forts also guarded the harbor: the Island Battery at the mouth and the Grand Battery facing the harbor entrance.

Most of the forts in North America were simple rectangular or star-shaped stockades made of logs placed upright in the ground. If the builders had time, they might erect a stronger wall using a framework of beams filled

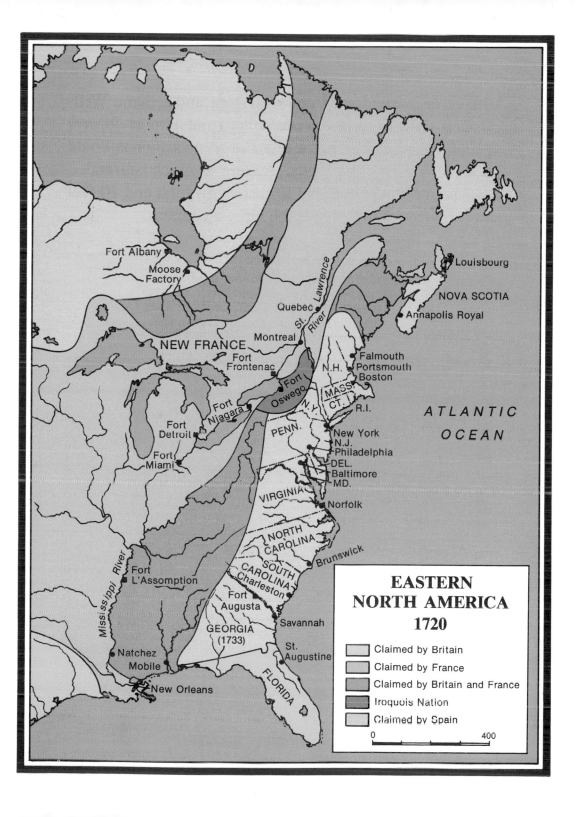

Fort Albany

Moose
Factory

Quebec

St. Lawrence River

Montreal

NEW FRANCE

Fort
Frontenac

Fort
Oswego

Fort
Niagara

Fort
Detroit

Fort
Miami

Louisbourg

NOVA SCOTIA

Annapolis Royal

Falmouth
N.H.   Portsmouth
Boston

MASS.

CT.   R.I.

N.Y.

PENN.

New York
N.J.
Philadelphia
DEL.
Baltimore
MD.

VIRGINIA

Norfolk

NORTH
CAROLINA

Brunswick

Mississippi River

Fort
L'Assomption

SOUTH
CAROLINA
Charleston

Fort
Augusta

GEORGIA
(1733)

Savannah

St.
Augustine

FLORIDA

Natchez
Mobile

New Orleans

ATLANTIC
OCEAN

EASTERN
NORTH AMERICA
1720

Claimed by Britain

Claimed by France

Claimed by Britain and France

Iroquois Nation

Claimed by Spain

0   400

with earth and perhaps faced with stone and cement. Well-manned wilderness forts could hold out almost forever against Indian raids, but a few European cannons could knock holes in their walls, forcing a quick surrender. Louisbourg's stone walls—30 feet (9 m) high and 10 feet (3 m) thick—defied all but the largest cannons.

A detailed colonial map shows the French fortress city of Louisbourg, built on Cape Breton Island to guard the entrance to the vital St. Lawrence River. For unknown reasons, the map was drawn with North toward the bottom of the page.

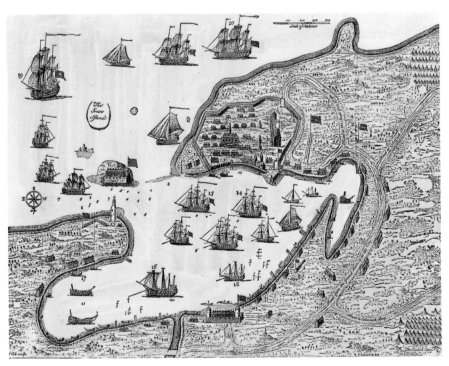

Cannons were rated according to the weight of the solid iron balls they fired. On the march, an army dragged along cannons ranging from 3-pounders to 12-pounders. Large warships mounted 24- or even 32-pounders. The Grand Battery at Louisbourg had awesome 42-pounders. Cannons were loaded from the open end—the muzzle—with bags of gunpowder and any of a variety of deadly projectiles. Solid shot was used against ships, fort walls, and distant troops. Fearsome sprays of musket balls, called grapeshot, tore apart ranks of charging infantry. Exploding shells—hollow balls filled with gunpowder—were lobbed over fort walls to kill defenders and set buildings afire.

In addition to stone walls and nearly 100 heavy guns, Louisbourg had strong natural defenses. Fog and high waves made a landing on Cape Breton Island difficult much of the year. Wide, sticky swamps protected the land approaches to the city. Yet Louisbourg had a great flaw: the size of its garrison. The city had only 700 soldiers, instead of the 3,000 it needed to man all the guns and walls, when news of another war in Europe arrived in the spring of 1744. This time the conflict would be called the War of the Austrian Succession in Europe, and King George's War in America (1744–1748).

The French at Louisbourg immediately prepared to invade Nova Scotia. What the French called Acadia had been in British hands since 1713. About 10,000 peasant farmers, originally from the French provinces of Brittany and La Rochelle, lived in the green, hilly land. Plain, uneducated people, the Acadians wanted little except to be left alone. Through the thirty years since the last war, they had stubbornly refused to listen to French priests or British army officers who demanded that they take sides in the rivalry between the two empires.

The French from Louisbourg struck before the handful of British soldiers in Nova Scotia even heard about the war. The French captured the small fishing port of Canso at the north end of the peninsula, then marched southwest to Annapolis Royal, the main British fort in Nova Scotia. A French priest added his band of local Micmac Indians to the attack, but 100 British soldiers put up a stout defense. When the Acadians refused to help, the French returned to Louisbourg.

Word of French attacks in Nova Scotia brought action by one of early America's great leaders, Governor William Shirley (1694–1771) of Massachusetts. Shirley talked the New England colonies into raising an army to capture Louisbourg. Command was given to William Pepperrell

Despite little military experience, Boston merchant William Pepperrell proved an exceptionally able commander of the New England army's "mad scheme" to capture Louisbourg.

LT. GEN. SIR WM. PEPPERRELL BART.
The Victor of Louisbourg A.D. 1745.

(1696–1759), a wealthy Boston merchant. Pepperrell had almost no military experience, but he was smart, determined, and popular. Some 4,000 men joined the expedition. Like their commander, most were beginners at war. What training they had came from service in the militia, a self-defense force called out to meet French and Indian raids. That the militiamen planned to storm the high walls of Louisbourg against cannons manned by well-trained French regulars was, in the words of the historian Francis Parkman, "a mad scheme."

Pepperrell's army got underway from Boston in March 1745. Crammed into fishing boats and small trading ships, the soldiers suffered through a stormy voyage to Nova Scotia. Commodore Peter Warren joined them at Canso with four Royal Navy warships to shut off Louisbourg from the sea. On April 30, boats began landing the army 2 miles (3.2 km) west of the fortress. For the next few days, American militiamen and British sailors wrestled supplies and equipment through the icy surf. The army lacked heavy cannons, and Pepperrell was trying to find another way to attack the city when a scouting party made an astonishing discovery: the Grand Battery facing the harbor entrance stood empty, its great 42-pounders almost undamaged!

Short of men, Louisbourg's commander had abandoned the battery, but his soldiers had failed to carry out orders to

On April 30, 1745, the New England army lands
on Cape Breton Island for a march across the
supposedly impassable swamps surrounding Louisbourg.

destroy the cannons. The French mistake gave the Americans more than enough firepower to blast holes in the city's walls, but first they had to get the cannons within range. Moving the heavy guns across the swamps proved a back-breaking task. The Americans loaded them on sledges 5 feet (1.5 m) wide and 16 feet (4.9 m) long. As many as 300 men harnessed themselves to the "stone boats" and dragged the cannons through waist-deep mud. In a re-

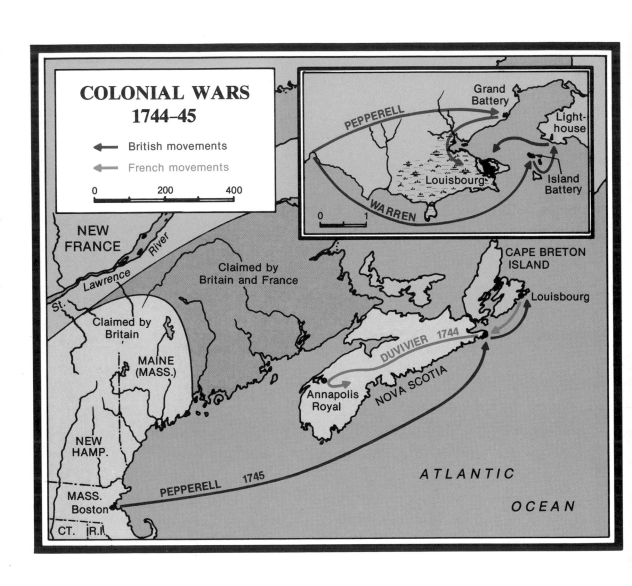

COLONIAL WARS 1744–45

← British movements
← French movements

0   200   400

NEW FRANCE

St. Lawrence River

Claimed by Britain and France

Claimed by Britain

MAINE (MASS.)

NEW HAMP.

MASS. Boston

CT. R.I.

Annapolis Royal

DUVIVIER 1744

NOVA SCOTIA

CAPE BRETON ISLAND

Louisbourg

PEPPERELL 1745

ATLANTIC OCEAN

Inset map

PEPPERELL

WARREN

Louisbourg

Grand Battery

Light-house

Island Battery

0   1

markable feat of muscle, grit, and skill, the Americans had the first cannons in position less than a week after the landing.

The cannons began firing on the city, setting buildings ablaze and knocking chunks of stone from the walls. Meanwhile, Pepperrell and Warren worried that a French fleet might come to Louisbourg's rescue. If Warren could get his ships inside the harbor, they could add their guns to the shelling. The Island Battery lay in the way. Four hundred men volunteered for a night attack. Before leaving shore, they fortified themselves with rum to ward off the cold and the fear. Undiscovered, they landed on the narrow island and started for the battery. Then a drunk gave a cheer, and the French woke to the danger. Cannons roared, muskets barked, and the Americans fell by the score. Nearly half the attackers were killed or captured.

Giving up the idea of a direct assault on the Island Battery, Pepperrell ordered cannons dragged to Light House Point across the harbor from the island. The American guns opened fire on June 10, forcing the French to abandon the battery. Warren's ships sailed into the harbor to join in blasting the city. With much of Louisbourg destroyed and its citizens cowering in cellars, the French commander surrendered on June 15. The Americans had succeeded in their mad scheme.

The siege cost the Americans 100 killed. Another 1,000 died of disease while holding the fortress until British soldiers arrived in the spring of 1746. The capture of Louisbourg became a source of great pride for the American colonies. After years of Indian raids and failed attacks on Canada, they finally had something to show for all their labor and blood. In 1748, France and Britain again made peace. To the disgust of the Americans, the British returned Louisbourg and Cape Breton Island to the French in exchange for land in far-off India. It was an insult that the Americans would never forget.

A CONTINENT IN THE BALANCE

IN THE spring of 1754, Lieutenant Colonel George Washington (1732–1799) led 120 Virginia militiamen into the wilderness to open the lands beyond the Appalachians for American settlement. Britain's colonies had changed immensely since the beginning of the Colonial Wars. With a booming population of well over a million, they were expanding rapidly westward. Many families had lived in the New World for generations and no longer thought of themselves as transplanted Europeans but as Americans. That summer, representatives of seven colonies met in Albany, New York. They adopted a plan advanced by Benjamin Franklin (1706–1790) to unite the colonies under a common government. Approval by the king would put America on the path to independence within the British Empire. But the colonial assemblies, jealous of their individual powers, overruled the Albany

Indian guides look on as Lieutenant Colonel
George Washington leads sabbath services during the
Virginia militia's 1754 march into
the Pennsylvania wilderness.

Congress. Franklin and America would have to wait a while longer.

The young Washington had little time to think about the future of America as his men started the hard march across the mountains. Governor Robert Dinwiddie (1693–1770) of Virginia had ordered him to build a fort at the Forks of the Ohio, where the Allegheny and Monongahela rivers join to form the wide Ohio River. A fort at the point where Pittsburgh, Pennsylvania, now stands would give Virginia control of the rich Ohio Valley and open a water route to the Mississippi. At twenty-two, the erect, muscular Washington was no stranger to this wild country. A year before, he had carried a message from Dinwiddie to Fort Le Boeuf on the Allegheny, demanding that the French leave the lands belonging to the British king. Le Boeuf's commander had answered that the Ohio Valley belonged to the French and that the colonists should stay on their own side of the Appalachians.

The French were prepared to fight for the Ohio Valley. For over a century, they had controlled the lakes and rivers of the north and the Mississippi flowing south to New Orleans and the Gulf of Mexico. The Ohio River sliced through the heart of this great fur-trading empire, and the French could ill afford to let American settlers into the valley. While Washington's little army cut a road through the wilderness, 1,000 French and Indians took the Forks of the Ohio and began building Fort Duquesne. Washington pushed on to Great Meadows near today's Uniontown, Pennsylvania, where he built Fort Necessity. A sharp fight with a band of Frenchmen camped nearby brought the French from Fort Duquesne. Washington's men took cover behind the crude walls of Fort Necessity under heavy fire from the woods. A drenching rain fell, filling the fort's trenches with muddy water and spoiling the American gunpowder. Outnumbered and nearly out of food, Washington surrendered when promised that he could take his men back to Virginia. It was a gloomy beginning to the career of the young man who would one day become "the father of his country."

This small fight in the wilderness began the final struggle between Britain and France for North America. To meet the French threat in the Ohio Valley, Britain sent an army under General Edward Braddock (1695–1755) to America. Few British regulars had served in America before. Untrained and unwilling to fight in the ways of the wilderness, the regulars expected to form their long red lines and wait for equally brave French regulars to meet them in a stand-up European-style fight.

Washington joined Braddock's staff as the heavily equipped army advanced on Fort Duquesne in the summer of 1755. The road the regulars built across the wilderness was a marvel, but it led to disaster. Ten miles (16 km) from Fort Duquesne, the British ran into heavy fire from French soldiers and Indians hidden in the woods. Surrounded on three sides, the regulars tried to pull back to form a line, but the withdrawal became tangled in the train of supply wagons. The battle turned into a slaughter, with nearly 1,000 of the proud regulars falling dead or wounded. Fortunately for the British, they had Washington. Taking over for the fatally wounded Braddock, Washington organized a retreat that brought the dazed and bleeding regulars out of the wilderness.

Although France and Britain were still at peace in Europe, the fighting spread quickly in America. That same

Bleeding from a mortal wound, General Edward Braddock
is taken from the scene of the disastrous
ambush in the Pennsylvania wilderness.

summer, Sir William Johnson (1715–1774) led an army of
3,500 Americans up the Hudson River. Johnson was a
remarkable man: a rich trader, a great friend of the Iroquois, and one of early America's most influential leaders.
Fifty miles (80 km) above Albany, his men built Fort
Edward, then crossed the long portage to Lake George,
where they began building Fort William Henry. To the
north lay Lake Champlain, the natural pathway for an
invasion of Canada. The French held Lake Champlain with

Firing from behind the unfinished walls of
Fort William Henry, Sir William Johnson's
New York militia takes a terrible toll on attacking
French and Indians at the Battle of Lake George.

a fort at Crown Point, manned by French regulars under
Baron Ludwig August Dieskau. Dieskau saw the threat and
struck first. His 1,500 regulars, Canadian militia, and
Indians caught 1,000 of Johnson's men on the march
and gave them a frightful beating. Thinking Johnson lay at
his mercy, Dieskau attacked Fort William Henry, but Johnson's cannons mowed down the attackers. The French re-
treated to Lake Champlain, where they built a fort to guard
the southern end of the lake. Called Fort Carillon by the
French and Fort Ticonderoga by the British, it would

become one of the most famous military sites in North America.

The French were also strengthening their fortress at Louisbourg on Cape Breton Island and stirring up trouble in Nova Scotia. A French priest led Indians and a few Acadians in raids on British outposts. When neutral Acadians failed to warn of the attacks, the British drove them from their homes. Many escaped to Canada, but some 6,000 were herded aboard ships and scattered from Massachusetts to Georgia. Eventually, some returned to Nova Scotia, while a few hundred made their way to French

Driven from their homes by the British, Nova Scotia's French Acadians embark on an uncertain future.

Shocked by the brutality of wilderness war,
the Marquis de Montcalm tries to stop a
massacre of prisoners by his Indian allies.

Louisiana where their descendants became the Cajuns of
today.

After two years of fighting in America, Britain declared
war on France in May 1756, opening a global conflict
called the Seven Years' War. In America, it became known
as the French and Indian War. That spring France sent a
great general to Canada. The Marquis de Montcalm
(1712–1759) was a small, energetic man with an extraor-
dinary talent for war. He set out to end the British threat to

New France's vital waterways. The British had built a new fort at the mouth of the Oswego River to open the Mohawk River route to Lake Ontario. Montcalm's army of regulars, Canadians, and Indians overpowered Fort Oswego. Unused to the hard ways of the wilderness, Montcalm neglected to protect his prisoners, and the Indians scalped and killed 100 of them.

Fort William Henry on Lake George became Montcalm's next target. In late July 1757, he brought 8,000 men—the largest army in the history of New France—south from Lake Champlain. Promised protection from the Indians, the garrison gave up after three days of siege, but the Indians brushed aside the thin guard of French regulars to kill some 150 prisoners before French officers and a priest managed to stop them.

With the fall of Fort William Henry, French power reached its height in North America, but one of the century's greatest men was determined to destroy New France once and for all. William Pitt (1708–1778) was the first British prime minister to understand that the fight in North America was not a sideshow to the European wars but a great struggle for the richest empire in history. Pitt issued orders to his generals for the summer of 1758. They were to take Fort Ticonderoga and Crown Point on Lake Champlain, Fort Duquesne at the Forks of the Ohio, Fort Frontenac on Lake Ontario, and of course, the greatest of them all, Louisbourg on Cape Breton Island. Gone were the days of short, savage fights between untrained foes in the wilderness. This would be war in the European style, with large regular armies fighting for final victory in America.

The British army met three of Pitt's goals in 1758. Lord Jeffrey Amherst (1717–1797) and a brilliant young general named James Wolfe (1727–1759) attacked Louisbourg. Their plan was almost the same as Pepperrell's in 1745, but this time it took 9,000 British regulars and 40 warships to take the mighty fortress. Far to the west, Colonel John Bradstreet (1711–1774) led a raid that destroyed Fort Frontenac almost without loss of life. To the south, a desperately ill General John Forbes (1710–1759) moved on Fort Duquesne, constructing a string of forts to guard his supply lines and leapfrogging his army forward. Almost within sight of the Forks of the Ohio, the British heard a great explosion as the French blew up the fort and scattered into the wilderness. Forbes died a few months later, as Fort Pitt rose on the rubble of Fort Duquesne.

All these successes were offset by a great disaster at Ticonderoga. Pitt had chosen unimaginative General James Abercromby (1706–1781) to open the invasion route into Canada along Lake Champlain. Some officers doubted Abercromby's ability to match the brilliant Montcalm, but they took comfort in Pitt's choice of the gifted Lord George Augustus Howe as second in command. In early July, Abercromby set out for Ticonderoga with the largest army yet seen on the continent. Nearly

Lord Jeffrey Amherst (center) discusses
the siege of Louisbourg with his brilliant
second in command, General James Wolfe (left).

1,000 boats carried 14,000 regulars, militiamen, and friendly Indians north over the calm waters of Lake Champlain toward the fort.

At Ticonderoga, Montcalm had fewer than 4,000 men. The fort could hold only a few hundred, so Montcalm decided to make a stand on the ridge across the narrow point of land behind the fort. On the Heights of Carillon, his men felled trees to build a high log wall. The crowns of the trees were left in a long tangle before the wall, their leaves stripped and branches sharpened in what was called an *abatis*, from the French word for "slaughterhouse."

The British army landed a few miles south of the fort on July 5, 1758. The next morning Howe led the advance through thick woods. In a sharp fight with a French company, the young general fell dead with a bullet through his heart. The loss stunned the army. The British returned to their boats and landed nearer the fort the following day. An inexperienced engineering officer reported to Abercromby that the French defenses on the Heights of Carillon could be taken without the help of cannon fire to knock holes in the *abatis* and the log wall. Abercromby did not bother to look for himself. From the safety of his headquarters well

Commander of General John Forbes's advance guard, Colonel George Washington plants the British flag on the ramparts of Fort Duquesne on November 25, 1758.

Ordered to attack across open ground against stout
defenses, British regulars and Scottish Highlanders
die in the murderous French fire from the Heights
of Carillon near Fort Ticonderoga on July 8, 1758.

to the rear, he ordered the attack on the morning of July 8.
The British regulars advanced across an open field straight
into the teeth of the French fire. They were chewed up and
thrown back. Four more times they charged. Scottish
Highlanders threw their muskets aside and tried to chop

through the *abatis* with their swords. The French shot them down in the slaughterhouse. After six terrible hours, the British fell back, leaving more than 1,600 dead and wounded on the field—more than four times the French losses. Cannons still unfired, the British army withdrew to the south.

Montcalm had won time, but New France was in a bad way by the spring of 1759. France's policy of keeping settlements lean and the fur trade fat left Canada with a population too small to protect or even to feed itself. The British navy choked off supplies from France. Montcalm's small army was stretched across hundreds of miles of frontier. Many of the Native American tribes sensed the defeat of New France and stayed clear of the war. While Montcalm labored to prepare his army for the summer's fighting, Prime Minister Pitt made the British plans. He fired the blundering Abercromby and gave Lord Jeffrey Amherst the task of taking Ticonderoga and pushing north along Lake Champlain into Canada. Meanwhile, General James Wolfe would bring a powerful army up the St. Lawrence to lay siege to Quebec.

Amherst was a careful man. A year after Abercromby's defeat, he landed his army near Ticonderoga. Woods-wise light infantry and the famed American rangers of Major Robert Rogers (1731–1795) swept the forest for Indians while the regulars rolled cannons into position to shell the

Lord Jeffrey Amherst watches Fort Ticonderoga
burn on July 26, 1759.

fort. Before the cannons could open fire, the small French
garrison blew up the fort and took to the water. Amherst
moved north to find Crown Point burned and empty. He set
about repairing the forts and building warships. The task
took well into September. By then, there was news from
Quebec.

In late June 1759, the unmatched seamen of the British

navy brought 22 warships and 119 transports up the tricky waters of the St. Lawrence to anchor beneath the high bluff of Quebec. General James Wolfe and 9,000 regulars had come to take the capital of New France. Only thirty-two, Wolfe was a tall, cold, friendless man. In poor health and almost constant pain, Wolfe drove himself hard as he prepared for the grim task ahead. Atop a 200-foot (60-m) cliff, the city of Quebec stood protected by thick walls and scores of cannons. To the east, the swift Montmorency River formed another barrier. Montcalm had 2,500 regulars and some 10,000 militia and friendly Indians to keep the British from climbing the bluff or crossing the Montmorency. Time was also on Montcalm's side. By October, the British ships would have to sail down the St. Lawrence ahead of the autumn gales, taking Wolfe's army along or leaving it to starve.

Wolfe placed cannons on the south side of the St. Lawrence and began shelling the city while his army landed to the east of the Montmorency. Montcalm ignored the damage to the city and camped most of his army at Beauport, on the west side of the Montmorency, to block a British crossing. For weeks Wolfe tested the French defenses but could find no weakness. His soldiers suffered bloody losses while the French held stubbornly to their positions. Montcalm refused to meet the British in an open-field battle where Wolfe's regulars would have the edge.

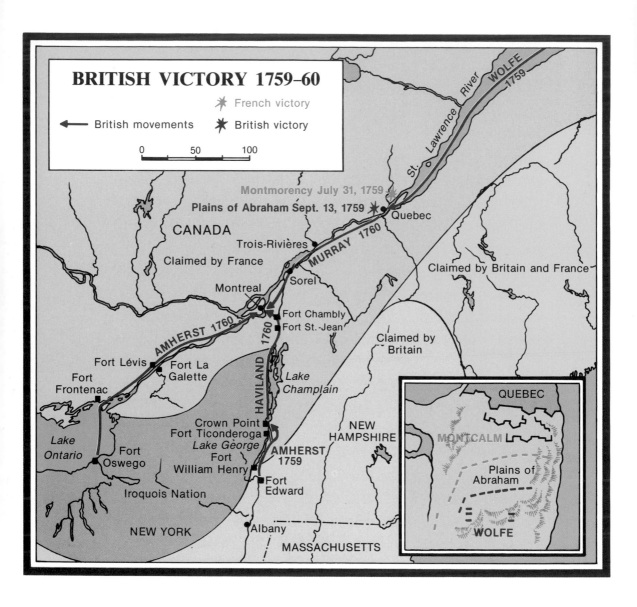

BRITISH VICTORY 1759–60

✳ French victory

← British movements ✳ British victory

0   50   100

St. Lawrence River   WOLFE 1759

Montmorency July 31, 1759 ✳

Plains of Abraham Sept. 13, 1759 ✳

Quebec

CANADA

Trois-Rivières   MURRAY 1760

Claimed by France

Sorel

Montreal   Claimed by Britain and France

Fort Chambly

AMHERST 1760   Fort St.-Jean

HAVILAND 1760

Fort Lévis   Fort La   Claimed by

Galette   *Lake*   Britain

Fort   *Champlain*

Frontenac

Crown Point   NEW

Fort Ticonderoga   HAMPSHIRE

Lake   *Lake George*   AMHERST

Ontario   Fort   1759

Fort   William Henry

Oswego   Fort

Iroquois Nation   Edward

NEW YORK   Albany

MASSACHUSETTS

QUEBEC

MONTCALM

Plains of
Abraham

WOLFE

Chill September mornings brought the first hints of fall to Quebec. Tired and depressed, Wolfe called his senior officers together. They planned a final attempt to capture the city. Admiral Charles Saunders agreed to take the army another dozen dangerous miles upriver for a landing to the west of Quebec. Bad weather delayed the landing, further dampening the army's spirits. Then Wolfe spotted something that had escaped other eyes—a narrow cove at the cliff base only 1.5 miles (2.4 km) west of the city. He made a bold decision. On the night of September 12, Wolfe led a line of darkened boats into what would ever after be called Wolfe's Cove. A challenge rang out from the top of the cliff. While the men in the boats held their breath, a French-speaking British officer answered it. "Pass friends," came the reply. The boats scraped the rocky beach. The first men scrambled up the cliff, leaping out of the darkness to stab and club the French guards. In a few minutes, the top of the cliff was in British hands.

Dawn found a long line of red-coated British regulars forming on the Plains of Abraham to the west of the city. Montcalm rushed to the scene from his camp at Beauport. He had about 4,500 men at hand; Wolfe perhaps 3,300. Montcalm prepared to attack. As the French regulars and militia fell into line, snipers in the woods fired into the British ranks. The British regulars stood stiffly at attention, their muskets double-loaded and long bayonets gleaming. When a soldier fell, the man behind stepped

On the night of September 12, 1759,
General James Wolfe climbs to the Plains of
Abraham where the British and French would
fight the decisive battle of the Colonial Wars.

forward to take his place. Armed only with a cane, Wolfe strolled along the ranks, smiling and joking with the men. A sniper's bullet shattered his wrist, but he paused only long enough to have it bound with a handkerchief. The French advanced, drums beating and flags flying. At 130 yards (120 m), they loosed a ragged fire. British soldiers fell, but the long ranks held their fire. The French fired again, then again. It seemed that Wolfe would never give the order to reply. With the French lines only 40 yards (37 m) away, he brought his cane down and fire leaped from the British muskets. The French ranks melted under the murderous volley. The British charged to finish the work with bayonets.

Shot in the lungs and stomach, Wolfe lay in the arms of an officer. He managed to ask how the battle was going. Told that the French were running, he smiled: "God be praised, I will die in peace."

The French left 1,400 dead and wounded on the field, more than twice the British losses. Shot through the body,

On the Plains of Abraham, outside New France's capital of Quebec, Wolfe's British army routs Montcalm's French forces on September 13, 1759.

Wounded three times, General James Wolfe
dies in the arms of his officers.

Montcalm clung to his horse. Back in the city, a doctor
uncovered the terrible wound and told him that it was fatal.
Montcalm replied: "So much the better. I will not see the
surrender of Quebec."

The fall of Quebec four days later signaled the end of
France's empire in North America. In the spring of 1760,
the French tried to retake the city but were driven off. That
summer, General Amherst sent three armies by way of
Lake Champlain, Lake Ontario, and the St. Lawrence

River to capture Montreal, the last Canadian city of importance in French hands. Peace came to America. Three years later, the treaty ending the Seven Years' War gave all of New France except Louisiana to Great Britain.

Victory made the British Empire the world's largest and most powerful, but its rule in America lasted only twenty years. No longer fearing the French, the American colonies quarreled with Britain. The long years of war had made the

British troops drill in the shadow of
Quebec Cathedral following the surrender
of New France's capital. But British
rule in North America would end
when the thirteen colonies
declared their independence.

Americans into a proud and self-reliant people. In 1776, the thirteen colonies declared their independence. George Washington and many veterans of the struggle against the French and the Indians joined the fight for liberty. The Iroquois sided with the British, only to be crushed by the Americans. For another century, Native Americans would fight a losing battle as white settlers pushed west toward the Pacific. The Americans would try to take Canada during the Revolution and again in the War of 1812, but Canada—including the largest French population outside of France itself—remained loyal to Great Britain, eventually following a peaceful path to independence within the empire.

Today tourists visit Ticonderoga, Louisbourg, Fort Necessity, Deerfield, and the Plains of Abraham, but most of the battlegrounds of those distant wars are forgotten. Yet the experience of the clashes in the wilderness lies deep in the American memory. In the long struggle, we felt the first stirrings of nationhood and sensed for the first time our possibilities for greatness as an independent people.

THE FLINTLOCK MUSKET

THE COLONIAL Wars were fought with the flintlock musket. A soldier carried paper-wrapped ammunition in a cartridge pouch slung at his side. To load his musket, he tore the end of a cartridge with his teeth and sprinkled gunpowder into the pan of the firing mechanism, where it would be set off by a spark when the piece of flint on the hammer struck the steel latch covering the pan. He then pushed the rest of the cartridge into the open end of the barrel and jammed the powder and lead ball down with a long steel rod called a ramrod. Despite the lengthy procedure, an expert could fire three or four shots a minute.

The standard British Brown Bess musket was some 5 feet (1.5 m) long, weighed 10 pounds (4.5 kg), and fired a ball of more than 1 ounce (28 g). Although accurate only to about 75 yards (67.5 m), it was a particularly deadly weapon in the hands of infantrymen firing in tight ranks.

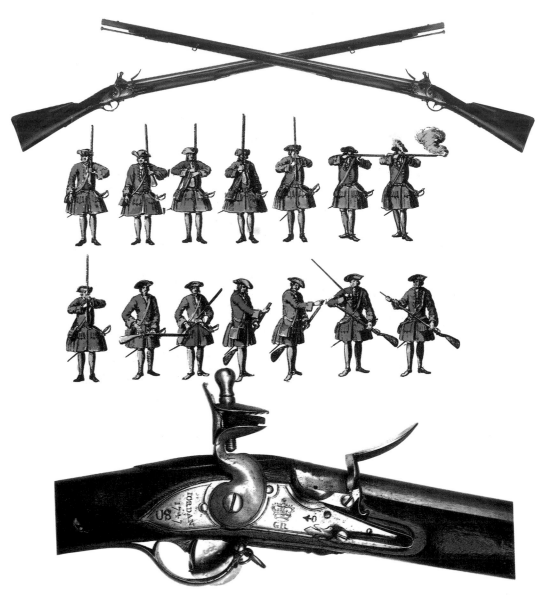

After two or three volleys, the ranks usually charged to finish the battle with the 21-inch (53.5-cm) bayonets fixed to the end of their muskets.

SUGGESTED READING

Downey, Fairfax. *Louisbourg: Key to a Continent*. Englewood Cliffs, N.J.: Prentice-Hall, 1965.

Hamilton, Edward P. *The French and Indian Wars*. Garden City, N.Y.: Doubleday, 1962.

Peckham, Howard H. *The Colonial Wars: 1689–1762*. Chicago: University of Chicago Press, 1964.

Roberts, Kenneth L. *Northwest Passage*. Garden City, N.Y.: Doubleday, 1937. (Fiction)

Smith, Bradford. *Rogers' Rangers and the French and Indian War*. New York: Random House, 1956.

William, Barry. *The Struggle for North America*. New York: McGraw-Hill, 1967.

INDEX

ABOUT THE AUTHOR

ALDEN
satile writer for children
nonfiction books on
Illinois, Shoshoni
the Alamo, the B
lution, the War of 18
and the Spanish-America
son (1984), *Wart, Son of i*
(1987), and *Up Country* (1989) w
can Library Association's annual li
Young Adults. His fifth novel, *RoboDad*,
Children's Fiction Book of 1990 by the Society
Authors. Mr. Carter lives with his wife, Carol,
children, Brian Patrick and Siri Morgan, in Marsh
Wisconsin.